LIFE LESSONS, VOL. 1 - 47 TIPS TO TRANSCEND YOUR EDUCATION

BAYODE OKUSANYA

First paperback edition March 2021

Book design by Alyssa Nguyen

ISBN 979-8-7172-8348-9 (paperback)

www.bayoofficial.com

CONTENTS

Bayo is an investor, entrepreneur, and creator.

He graduated from Princeton University in 2020, where he majored in Philosophy and earned a certificate in Entrepreneurship. He is the first hire of Chaac Ventures, an early-stage venture capital firm focused on the Princeton University tech ecosystem.

During his freshman year at Princeton, Bayo was the Financial Coordinator of Princeton Envision: a non-profit that brought together innovators, engineers, scientists, business leaders, intellectuals and policy makers to discuss new technologies. Afterwards, Bayo became a co-founder and Chief Financial Officer of Princeton Empower, a group under Princeton's Entrepreneurship Club which promoted financial literacy among college students, especially those from low-income backgrounds. He also worked as an associate with Princeton University's e-Lab Accelerator, where he supported Princeton startups and first-time founders.

During his final year at Princeton, Bayo became the Vice President of Finance for the Africa Summit at Princeton initiative, where he helped develop the first New Venture competition for African startups on Princeton's campus and received the Africa Summit Fellowship.

Today, Bayo supports startup founders and future venture capitalists on and off Princeton's campus.

I wrote this handbook with my generation – Generation Z – in mind, to help them overcome the "generational curses" that held back those before us, so we can rise to this moment in history.

Thank you to all the friends, mentors, and heroes who I've watched closely to learn these lessons. I'd also like to thank the anti-heroes as well, who's bad behavior I've learned a great deal from.

Most importantly, I'd like to thank my parents, Olajide and Kate Okusanya, who brought my siblings and me to this country from Nigeria, when I was only two years old. And to my sister, Olusayo Okusanya, and my brother, Kolade Okusanya, thank you for all the wisdom you've passed down to me over the years. All of your sacrifices have forever changed the course of my life and will impact generations of our family to come. Words cannot express how appreciative I am for all you've done for me. Thank you, thank you, thank you, and God bless.

. . .

(FINALLY, thank you Alyssa Nguyen for helping me with the cover art for the book. Your design skills are awesome and inspiring.)

Ecclesiastes 9:11, NIV:
"I have seen something else under the sun:
The race is not to the swift
or the battle to the strong,
nor does food come to the wise
or wealth to the brilliant
or favor to the learned;
but time and chance happen to them all."

Before starting on your journey, you should know that there are several levels of understanding and application along the way. There's "levels to this" is really an understatement, but it helps describe the depth of wonder and beauty this life has to offer. Each level in life helps filter out our worst characteristics (if you're doing it right), so we can become the best versions of ourselves through continuous growth. Don't shy away from life just because it seems tough on the surface. Experience it for yourself. Think deeply about it on your own terms. Jump in and never look back. You won't regret it.

The following pages are a collection of lessons I learned during the first chapter of my life journey. Following in the footsteps of Ray Dalio, author of Principles and Founder of Bridgewater Associates, I decided to record each lesson I learned along the way in real time. My intention is to help others avoid the same mistakes I made, so you can move full speed ahead towards your dreams.

There are 47 lessons in this book. I understand that some things in this book will seem obvious to many successful people who are well on their way to achieving their life's purpose. This book is not intended to help the already successful. It's intended to help the youth overcome the struggles of balancing their education and life, and also help anyone who is lost and in search of answers. I hope this book provides you a beacon of hope.

If you haven't heard it before, let me be the first to tell you: I have full faith in you and everything you hope to accomplish. May God be with you.

LESSON 1: YOUR STRENGTH OF CHARACTER IS MORE IMPORTANT THAN YOUR GPA

*Y*our GPA is an imperfect indicator of how successful you will be. It measures how well you can follow old systems. It's predicated on the belief that those same systems will provide for your success in the future. The post-2020 world has shown us that nothing guarantees success more than your strength of character.

THE ORIGINAL HALF-TRUTH we're told when we enter the American education system is that our grades and GPA will decide our trajectory in life. I graduated Princeton University with a GPA I'm not proud of (in hindsight). It was certainly lower than my parent's expectations of me and the track record I had built up in high school and earlier.

At the time, I was terrified that I was letting everyone down. When I first entered Princeton University, I had built a stellar profile as a rising black engineer, and I had the accolades and the co-signs to prove it. I was awarded the African American Future Achievers Award by the Ronald McDonald

House Charities organization, and I was part of the first cohort of Robert F. Smith's Fund II Foundation S.T.E.M. Scholar's program.

At a certain point during my first year in college, I realized I was living a lie, that I did not want to be an engineer for real, nor was I willing to put in the work necessary. The truth was all I wanted to do was get to the end of the road, where I could kick my feet up and be a technical co-founder of a billion-dollar startup just like the entrepreneurs I looked up to.

But there are no shortcuts in this life, everything's a process.

I didn't understand that back then, so I railed against the systems around me and felt defeated and drained by a world I felt didn't truly understand me as an individual. I had a rough time because I was attempting to do something that had no precedent: crafting a personal legend built uniquely for Bayode Okusanya.

During my early years at Princeton, I was uninterested in structured education, and I was looking for answers to bigger questions about life and the world that I felt the traditional university system was not providing. I left the beaten path pretty early-on and I was very scared I wouldn't make it. I eventually did, but not for the reasons I was told would be most important.

I made it because I did unusual things like focusing most of my time on meeting interesting people, connecting with alumni and building great relationships with them, and carving out a path based on Philosophy and Entrepreneurship that produced a set of experiences unique to me and how I personally learn – by *doing*. It turns out that even in those moments when we're frustrated and things seem meaningless, life is trying to tell you something that reflects bigger truths about the reality all around us. All we have to do is pay closer attention to the lessons revealed in each moment.

The good news is that the world where a person's trajectory can be quantified with numbers alone is long gone. Who *you* are and the story you have to tell is the most important thing you can leverage. Don't ever take it for granted. You're more capable than you can even imagine.

LESSON 2: A GREAT BELIEF SYSTEM WILL LIFT UP EVERYONE AROUND YOU

good belief system produces good results in the world. It can be tested and applied to your own life and you can see for yourself how the "magic" works. However, a *great* belief system will produce results that not only outpace your wildest imaginations but also lifts up everyone around you as well.

IF YOU FIND that your belief system is not helping you grow, or is keeping you stagnated, then that's a sign that something needs to change.

ONE OF THE first things I learned was that you're allowed to test the systems given to us at birth. You're allowed to ask questions and you're allowed to seek your own answers. Not only that, but you can also learn even quicker by listening to other people and applying the lessons they've learned. It's good to seek other perspectives and then test things out for yourself. Never take someone else's word for it without doing your own research and introspection.

LESSON 3: IN THE WORDS OF BRUCE LEE: "BE LIKE WATER"

Be adaptable and flexible, especially in stressful times.

YOU NEVER KNOW how events will play out in your life, or whether something that looks or feels bad right now could actually be amazing for you one day. I've learned that a bad period is usually just a "stepping stone" to something greater. It doesn't mean it won't hurt, sometimes terribly. But it's nothing to be demoralized about. Hard times build strength.

LESSON 4: WE REAP WHAT WE SOW, PROPORTIONALLY

A small transgression will reap a small punishment. A large transgression will reap a large punishment. The same is true about how much you decide to give and what you receive in return from the world. It's all about whether you're giving proportionally more or proportionally less as you grow.

PEOPLE CAN TELL when a rich person is only donating a small part of their wealth to appease the masses. We can also tell if a poor person is donating a proportionally large amount of their wealth, even though it looks small to others. As long as you continue to sow proportionally, based on the level you're on, you'll continue to reap positive rewards indefinitely.

LESSON 5: IT'S ALRIGHT IF YOU CHANGE YOUR MIND ABOUT BIG DECISIONS

It's fine to give up on a life path you once thought was a good fit for you, as long as you never ever give up on yourself. EVER. This is crucial.

THE WORLD NEEDS you and your contributions. We need your ideas and your perspective. We don't have all the answers, even though many adults pretend like they do.

NO ONE HAS every piece to this puzzle. People can only give you what they know, based on their own life experiences, and that will never perfectly map onto another person's life.

DO what resonates with you for as long as it does. If you evolve and those same things no longer resonate, then feel free to re-align yourself with new activities. Trust me, your friends and family will understand and support you. That's what *unconditional love* is all about.

. . .

IT'S good to adjust and recalibrate until you find the lifestyle that's just right for you and pushes you towards the goals you want to achieve.

THE CLOSER YOUR goals align with your inner voice, or your *spirit*, the easier it is to focus only on the things that serve your goals. That's because your inner voice is the truest, most durable part about you, so it's easier to maintain the actions and goals that speak to that part of you directly.

BE careful of betraying that inner voice for material gain. That's the fastest way to lose your *spirit* and your motivation to want to get up and get active, each and every day.

LESSON 6: CONTINUOUSLY FEED YOUR MIND, BODY, AND SPIRIT IN A BALANCED WAY

A lack of balance will drain your energy, and will not do you any good, nor anyone around you. The journey towards your highest ideals is a marathon, not a sprint, and will require you to endure many obstacles along the way. The less balanced you feel, the harder it will be to make it to the next stage of life.

LUCKILY, you're not in this alone.

IF YOU'D LIKE to check out any of the things that I use to help stay balanced, you can visit my Amazon store and see what works for you: amazon.com/shop/bayo_de

LESSON 7: LEAD WITH YOUR "WHY"

Why are you taking this path versus some other one?

THE WORLD desperately wants to know who *you* are - not the person you think we want to see.

THE WORLD NEEDS real individuals who can manage themselves and bring fresh perspectives to the global debate. Your story is one of your most important resources. Leverage it. It's *yours* for a reason.

LESSON 8: ENCOURAGE OTHERS AND LISTEN TO THE VISION THEY HAVE FOR THEMSELVES

*L*isten to their passion, and if it really resonates with you, be the one person in a chorus of thousands who decides to bet on that person. When they one day reach their goal, you'll be one of the first people they'll call to celebrate.

OFTENTIMES, good energy is enough to sustain you, even if you're not the most talented. Good energy is infectious, and a word of encouragement is doubly so. Don't join the "haters."

LESSON 9: YOU DON'T NEED TO "CHASE THE BAG"

*W*ho really cares how much is in your bank account?

THE WORLD where what you have supersedes who *you* are is over and done with. Now, being *yourself* is greater than any currency imaginable. You'll stick out everywhere you go, and if you imbue *yourself* in all your work – from your essays, to your writing, to your social media posts – then the people who love you just for being *you* will come and find you.

CENTRAL to who *you* are is your life's purpose, so the earlier you can find it and do everything you can to achieve it, the more the world will work in your favor.

WHEN YOU'RE NOT sure about your purpose, it can change quickly with the seasons – which is why I advocate creating a general mission statement for your life, and then fill your life with activities that align with that mission statement.

From a very young age, I asked for *wisdom*. I wanted God to develop me into one of the wisest men to have ever lived, so I could positively impact countless lives. Today on my bedside wall, my "Statement of Purpose" reads: "Positively impact over a billion lives."

I didn't know back then what that meant in practice, was overcoming obstacle after obstacle, struggle after struggle, until finally the lessons stuck permanently.

It was a painful process, but one I wouldn't trade for the world. It's important to mentally prepare yourself for the journey ahead. The good news is you already have everything you need to make it on your journey. It was encoded in your DNA at birth.

LESSON 10: THINK LONG TERM. MAKE LONG TERM PLANS WITH LONG TERM PEOPLE

"*L*ong term people" are usually the individuals who align with your life's purpose.

HONESTLY, there are people I love who I cannot spend a lot of time with, not because I don't love them, but because nothing beats my life's purpose. I know that when they need me, they will seek me, and that's more than enough.

IT'S important to put your faith and energy into the things, values, and activities that will be important to you for the long run. It's a long life, and you don't want to waste it on anything that will turn against you eventually, or one day lose its luster.

LESSON 11: THERE ARE TWO TYPES OF PEOPLE IN THE WORLD: PEOPLE WHO CONSUME AND PEOPLE WHO PRODUCE

The more you can be a producer versus a consumer, the more prosperous your life will become.

IT WILL ALSO CHANGE the way you interact with the world. From other people's perspective, it will seem like you're dripping in blessings, always full of useful information and value. Hopefully, you choose to use your newfound power for good.

LESSON 12: IN THE REAL WORLD, THERE ARE MANY BAD FAITH ACTORS

*T*here are many people who only see the value you can offer them and who will not value you just for being a respectful human being. That's why you must learn to fight for your value.

AT MY CALMEST, I'm a non-confrontational person. I don't like to cause problems, but I understand I must fight.

So... I fight my battles in several ways:

- I fight by building relationships with powerful people who like *me* for *me*.
- I fight by sharing my perspective on the world and life through content on social media platforms.
- And finally, I fight by practicing righteousness in everything I do.

ALL OF THIS vouches for me when I'm not there to vouch for myself. It's very hard to defeat an *evolving target*.

LESSON 13: IMAGINE WHO YOUR BEST SELF COULD BE AND LIMIT YOUR EXPOSURE TO INFLUENCES THAT KEEP YOU FROM BECOMING HIM OR HER

Oftentimes, that person you imagine, at your highest elevation, is who you really should be – given enough time and energy to grow.

THAT PERSON ISN'T JUST a figment of your imagination. You can be him or her today. Right now. And I bet that's who your community needs you to be right now anyway. So, what are you waiting for?

THE TOUGHEST PART for me was dealing with a world that seemed committed to slowing me down at every turn. But that wasn't what was really happening. I lacked under-standing.

THE ONLY REASON it seemed slow was because I failed to understand that there was a process built into this life, and unless I learned how to follow the process of success, I'd keep finding it hard to obtain.

LESSON 14: LEARN HOW TO IGNORE THE OUTSIDE NOISE AND FOLLOW YOUR OWN INTERNAL COMPASS

The more you listen to that intuition, the better it becomes at getting you to the right answer quickly.

JUST MAKE sure you're feeding your mind with good information and positive sources, and your intuition can process the rest much quicker than you can currently imagine.

*M*ore often than not, if you give people enough slack, they'll reveal who they really are to you. Just wait on it.

EVERYTHING GOOD IS worth the wait, especially good friends and good relationships in life and work.

LESSON 16: BIG DREAMS ARE EXPENSIVE. YOU MUST BE WILLING TO PAY THE PRICE

The good news is: you will survive and it will provide you a unique story to tell.

I BELIEVE that within every person is a *big dreamer* waiting to emerge and contribute something positive and productive to the world. When you learn to direct the energy of your inner *dreamer* into activities that align with those big dreams, you become a force to be reckoned with.

HOWEVER, in order to avoid the negative consequences of some dreams, it's important to help other *dreamers* achieve their goals along the way. It will pay dividends later.

LESSON 17: BE STUBBORN ABOUT YOUR GOALS BUT FLEXIBLE ABOUT YOUR METHODS

In other words, maybe your goals aren't wrong, maybe your standards aren't too high, but maybe your *approach* to the problem needs to change.

WHEN YOU REALIZE that your approach is moving you further away from your goals than closer to them, there's an opportunity for change and growth there.

LESSON 18: GROW THROUGH WHAT YOU GO THROUGH

By simply observing the world, your thoughts, and your reactions to it, without internalizing everything negative that happens, you can learn the right lessons to *grow* past your current circumstances.

EVEN IF THE world around you is burning, it does not have to affect your peace.

LESSON 19: PUT YOURSELF IN A POSITION TO LEVEL UP

*I*n my experience, the easiest way to achieve my goals was by constantly leaving my comfort zone. When you leave your comfort zone, you find yourself in new situations where you can get lucky.

LEAVING my comfort zone helped me build the necessary experiences to get into Princeton University, get me my first internship, and get me my first job post-college. More importantly, it helped me build a reservoir of information that's very, very difficult to replicate, unless you've had my exact set of experiences.

DON'T BE afraid to reach out to that CEO you admire, or ask your crush on a date, or move to a new city you've never visited before.

. . .

GET COMFORTABLE WITH BEING UNCOMFORTABLE, and you will have the most unique life, built perfectly for *you*.

LESSON 20: RAISE YOUR SENSE OF RESPONSIBILITY FOR THE THINGS THAT HAPPEN IN YOUR LIFE

*Y*ou've probably heard of the phrase: "It takes two to tango."

IN SHORT, this phrase means that there's always multiple sides to every story, each with its own kernel of truth.

THE PROBLEMS that happen to us work much the same way: We often believe that the negative consequences we experience have nothing to do with us or our behavior, when in actuality we probably contributed to them in some way, shape, or form.

BY BUILDING A HIGHER sense of responsibility for your circumstances in life, you can begin to take your power back so you can overcome them.

LESSON 21: LEVERAGE YOUR PAIN
TO BUILD YOUR KINGDOM

*W*hen people inflict *pain* on you, they have no clue what they're really doing.

THEY'RE REALLY GIVING you all the motivation you need to go kick some ass.

FOR THE SAKE of argument though, let's imagine that you lived a life where everything flowed perfectly. There were never any roadblocks and it was all "sunshine and rainbows" from the day you were born.

WHAT WOULD you have to talk about, write about, or use to inspire others?

TO OTHER PEOPLE, you'll seem like an inexperienced child attempting to explain combat to decorated veterans.

. . .

YOU HAVE to experience hardships and fail sometimes, so you have the right lessons and wisdom to deliver to the next generation.

LESSON 22: BE WARY OF LETTING PEOPLE HAVE POWER OVER YOU

*E*specially, people who really, really want to have that power. That's an indicator that they may need further growth as a leader.

REAL LEADERS ATTRACT FOLLOWERS, rather than forcing others to follow them.

IT'S BETTER to put your faith in people's track records, but even that should be taken with a grain of salt. I'm personally biased towards waiting until you have strong conviction before moving forward with any action others prescribe for you.

LESSON 23: USE YOUR INEXPERIENCE TO YOUR ADVANTAGE BY SEEKING GUIDANCE FROM WISE MENTORS

A lot of older people might think you're some inexperienced kid. But if you're able to frame your inexperience right, seek advice, and listen attentively, then you can use that to your advantage.

THIS IS the exact email I sent to my mentor, friend, and employer, Luke Armour, when I first got in touch with him during my freshman year at Princeton:

SUBJECT: [AN INTRODUCTION] [PRINCETON UNIVERSITY STUDENT]

HELLO LUKE,

MY NAME IS BAYODE OKUSANYA. I attended your presentation last Wednesday, March 29th thanks to an invitation from a mutual friend of ours, Osagie Johnson. Thank you so much for coming to Princeton to share your mission and knowledge! It was a transformative and sincerely motivating talk for me.

WHEN WE SPOKE, I had mentioned that I had given myself a psuedo deadline to come up with and execute a startup idea by the end of summer. It only recently occurred to me that I am currently involved in a student organization under Princeton's Eclub that is on track to becoming an impactful startup. The name of the organization is Empower, and it is a movement to spread financial literacy to the Princeton campus, its neighboring communities, and eventually low income communities across the state and nation. I joined the organization around November last year as a cofounder after reading about its mission and connecting my experiences with that of the original founder. We both have been personally affected by the lack of financial literacy unfortunately prevalent among minorities and low income families: him as a first generation, low income student and me as an immigrant from Nigeria.

RIGHT NOW, Empower offers classes called "Empower Hours" to students on campus on a weekly basis, and we recently started offering classes with the Princeton Scholars Institute Fellows Program for low income, first generation students. The "Empower Hours" are currently the only product we offer as well as financial tips or advice if individuals want to reach out to us for help. We also just ran a campus wide survey to assess the campus' financial literacy that has received 488 responses to date; the data so far confirms our hypothesis that financial literacy is a dire need among students of all backgrounds.

. . .

Would you be able to link up to offer us guidance on how to turn what we currently have into a startup worthy of Chaac Ventures? We are particularly lacking in terms of a business model.

On a more personal note, it would be an honor to have your advice and wisdom on my journey as an entrepreneur. I am particularly interested in the Venture Capital business and potentially starting my own VC fund one day, but I am rudderless when it comes to breaking into the industry as a beginner and figuring out the landscape and its history. I'd appreciate the opportunity to learn from your own experience and journey to where you are today. Finally, are there any resources that you have personal experience with that you could point me towards to learn about venture capital and investment?

Thank you for your time!

Best regards,
Bayode Okusanya
Princeton University
Princeton Empower - Chief Financial Officer
Princeton Envision - Financial Coordinator

In hindsight, it was long-winded but it got the job done. And thankfully, it set off the necessary chain of events that lead me down the path to finding my true purpose. Feel free to adapt it and remember to keep your outreach emails short and to the point. Busy people appreciate short emails, especially during stressful times.

· · ·

IF YOU'D LIKE to read the full story of what happened after sending that email, you can read my blog posts on Medium: bayodeokusanya.medium.com

HERE'S the URL to my first blog post: https://bayodeokusanya.medium.com/where-to-start-when-youre-building-a-company-the-one-pager-aba6dc6fa523

LESSON 24: YOU ARE A CO-CREATOR OF YOUR OWN REALITY

*Y*ou create your reality through "paying" attention to the things that truly matter to you.

You HAVE a say about what you're going to pay attention to, so don't be afraid to focus only on the things that matter most to you.

YOUR ATTENTION IS a valuable currency that you do not have to give to just anyone. Choose wisely.

LESSON 25: GIVE FREELY AND OPENLY, WITHOUT PREJUDICE

One of the universal laws is essentially "what goes around, comes around." It's also known as karma. It's a very powerful concept if you observe your reality and see how what you put into it reflects back at you.

AVOID HAVING A "SELFISH ATTITUDE" when navigating your life and relationships. In other words, if you can create a life that helps others as a by-product, then you'll naturally attract good blessings.

LESSON 26: DEVELOP YOUR INTELLECTUAL PROPERTY

Intellectual property (IP) is all the art, writing, ideas, and more, that you develop yourself.

THE MORE IP YOU DEVELOP, the easier it becomes to develop more, as long as you continue taking care of your body, mind, and spirit.

IN MY OPINION, it's good practice to avoid selling the rights to your intellectual property. Intellectual property helps you build generational wealth so future generations of your family can have access to the income it produces.

LESSON 27: DEAL WITH LIFE FROM A POSITION OF STRENGTH

*I*f you're not feeling it today, it's alright to come back when you're ready.

YOUR REPUTATION IS A VERY valuable asset, and always showing up as your best self fortifies it.

A LOT of people may judge you based on your last effort without taking into account all the work you've put in up until now. Don't let that distract you.

KEEP MOVING FORWARD.

LESSON 28: GIVE CREDIT WHEREVER CREDIT IS DUE, AND NEVER TAKE CREDIT FOR THINGS YOU DIDN'T THINK OF FIRST

*I*f you share an idea, and others tell you that you're not the first to think of it, then it's important to let the original authors share in the victory. It's good form and saves you from a mob of angry supporters.

More importantly, avoid having a "boastful attitude," meaning constantly talking about yourself and your contributions. It's better to remain humble and approachable; you never know who is watching and how much impact you could have on others through a little patience and modesty. Not to mention how much joy you can spread by sharing the credit and praise from a job well done.

LESSON 29: EXPERIENCE IS A HIGHER LEVEL OF COMPREHENSION THAN READING OR LISTENING ALONE

A lot more information than you may be aware of is being transmitted when you experience something. It engages all of your five senses in a way that speaks particularly to you, based on your own life experiences.

THAT'S WHY PEOPLE SAY: "some things can't be taught". It's true. Not everything about life can be communicated in a classroom.

EXPLORE the world and come equipped with your own questions.

LESSON 30: TO OVERCOME A BIG
TASK, BREAK IT DOWN INTO
SMALLER PIECES AND THEN FOCUS
ON MAKING EACH OF THE SMALLER
PIECES EXCELLENT

At the end of the process, the sum of the parts will be much greater than the whole.

TO TAKE IT A STEP FURTHER, if you can tie each piece back into the overall theme in a way that makes sense, then when you put everything back together, the whole thing will seem well-planned.

THIS IS a trick that works with procrastination, but also with creative work like song writing or music production. Divide and conquer.

LESSON 31: GOOD HABITS ARE YOUR BEST FRIEND

The best way to build a good habit is through consistent practice. Practice daily and the results will compound exponentially. By the time you wake up from your daily practice, you'll see that no one around you can compete.

MOREOVER, constant practice helps you build good habits, and building good habits will help you build good character, which is more predictive of your future success than your GPA or your grades. A good person will continue to put themselves in good situations which will continue to produce good outcomes.

LESSON 32: BE WARY OF "ENEMIES OF YOUR SUCCESS"

"*E*nemies of your success" are people who are more angry about *what you stand for* than they are angry at *you.* If they were to meet you in person, they probably wouldn't think you're such a bad person.

To QUALIFY, I do not mean to say that you are any better than these people. Just that you're better off not engaging with them unless they're complaint is substantial and can be used to improve your work for the better.

LESSON 33: IF YOU HAVEN'T FOUND YOUR PASSION YET, OR YOUR LIFE'S PURPOSE, THEN DON'T STOP SEARCHING UNTIL YOU DO

The ultimate key to sustained success is getting paid to do activities you would do for free. When I was having trouble discovering my purpose, I had to do a lot of deep reflection back to my childhood and the things which came naturally to me.

I FOUND that philosophy and creativity were my strong suits, so I started focusing on the activities that would keep paying dividends in those areas.

LESSON 34: IMITATE SUCCESSFUL PEOPLE UNTIL YOU CAN DEFINE SUCCESS FOR YOURSELF

*B*y the time you come up with your own definition of success, you would have absorbed an arsenal of good characteristics from those heroes.

Now, you have everything you need to eventually surpass them. Just make sure that when you do, you pay homage to all the heroes who helped you along the way.

LESSON 35: YOUR CREATIVE AND EMOTIONAL ENERGY IS ONE OF YOUR MOST VALUABLE RESOURCES

*Y*our employers will desperately want it, so they can compete with other companies in the marketplace, through innovative products, inventions, strategies, and business models originated by their most creative employees.

IF YOU CAN USE that energy to build your own ventures as well, then your success will multiply exponentially.

LESSON 36: BEWARE THE "RAT RACE"

The "rat race" is the 9-5 job market for low wages. If you're not using your job to save up money and improve your craft so you can start your own venture, then you may get locked into a routine that leads to *stagnation*, or slow growth.

THE GOAL IS to break out of this cycle so you can pursue your true purpose to your heart's content. Thankfully, there's now several ways for you to build a business online to help you save up and master your craft even quicker. Check out <u>side-hustlestack.co</u>

LESSON 37: KEEP IN MIND THAT COMPANIES ALL OVER THE WORLD ARE COMPETING FOR YOUR ATTENTION

*R*emember, your attention is a valuable commodity nowadays, which means that by giving things your attention, you're giving away a priceless resource.

IT'S BETTER to focus most of your attention on the most important things in your life. In my opinion, these things are: God, Purpose, and Family.

LESSON 38: LIMIT NEGATIVE FEEDBACK LOOPS THAT EXIST AROUND YOU

Sometimes that means limiting your exposure to certain people, certain social media personalities, or anything that keeps you from pursuing your highest ideals.

THERE WILL BE plenty of time for these things once you're well on your way to achieving what you're here on Earth to achieve.

LESSON 39: FILLING UP YOUR MIND
WITH MORE INFORMATION THAN
YOU NEED, DOESN'T MEAN YOU'RE
GETTING SMARTER OR MAKING
PROGRESS

Progress comes from applied action.

CYCLE BETWEEN GETTING information you need and *applying* that information consistently to improve your life. When you can discern which information is necessary to achieve your purpose, you're well on your way to achieving mastery over your corner of the universe.

LESSON 40: LEARN TO WORK HARD FOR YOURSELF BEFORE YOU CAN WORK HARD FOR OTHERS

*I*n other words, become the type of person who can tare care of themself, before you go out and try to take care of the world. If you're in good standing with your own personal ideals and goals, then it will be much easier to help others find their way. They can learn from your experience.

IT HELPS when your goals for yourself align with how best you can serve others. That's when things will naturally click for you and supporters will come out of nowhere to contribute to what you're building. Most importantly, it frees your conscience so you can run toward your goals with fewer mental hurdles along the way.

LESSON 41: VIEW EVERYONE AROUND YOU AS POTENTIAL TEAMMATES AND NOT COMPETITORS

By doing so, you'll generate a better attitude towards others so you can continue focusing on your own goals and ideals without the mental stress that comes from trying to compete with everyone around you.

LESSON 42: DON'T DWELL ON THE PAST BECAUSE IT NO LONGER MATTERS

What matters is what you're doing right now to improve your future.

PERSONALLY, if I do think about the past, I do so for two reasons:

- To avoid the mistakes of past generations.
- To remember fallen loved ones.

LESSON 43: YOU ARE THE SUM TOTAL OF THE STORIES YOU TELL YOURSELF EVERY DAY

*E*very intention, every thought, every piece of content you absorb, affects the end product that is *you*. The good news is that you can change the stories you're telling yourself at any time, which will change everything about you as well.

AN EASY HACK TO change your internal storyline is to throw yourself into activities you would not traditionally associate with your identity. Your instincts should take over as you begin to adapt yourself to new situations. You'll learn more about yourself the more you witness the way you tend to handle unfamiliar territory.

LESSON 44: THE SECRET IS THAT THERE IS NO SECRET

One of the mistakes I made along my journey was believing that there was a "secret" to success. As a result, I kept searching for the *key* that would finally unlock the future I dreamed for myself. In actuality, the *key* was in my hands all along; I just needed to give myself permission to carefully plan my future.

TODAY, I believe the time I spent searching would have been better spent planning. I also learned that most people are taking things one day at a time and figuring things out little by little. The true Masters of this reality are focused on improving their craft(s) as often as they can, day-by-day.

LESSON 45: DELAYED GRATIFICATION IS KEY

Reward yourself only after you've finished what you need to get done. If you get into the habit of rewarding yourself too early, you may lose motivation to complete tasks to the best of your ability.

LESSON 46: TO BE A GREAT LEADER, THE FIRST PERSON YOU NEED TO LEARN HOW TO LEAD IS YOURSELF

One of the most important lessons I learned along my journey came from my brother, Kolade Okusanya. He taught me that "the only person we can really control is ourselves."

IT TURNS out that truly great leaders are chosen by others, not the other way around. True leaders are in control of themselves and their output. They value the quality of their work over the quantity.

IN SHORT, it's the *quality of their character* that attracts followers to them.

GROW into the person you're supposed to be and your followers will naturally find you.

LESSON 47: LIVE IN HARMONY WITH YOUR OWN PERSONAL NATURE AND THE NATURAL WORLD

*L*earn the natural laws that govern reality, so you don't accidentally fall into the same traps that hindered past generations.

THIS BOOK HAS elements of the natural laws imbued in it, but it's definitely not a comprehensive list. There's always more work that can be done and more work we can do to improve ourselves and our communities.

THE BEST WAY TO learn the natural laws is to live your life and learn something new every day.

GOOD LUCK ON YOUR JOURNEY, and may God be with you. Always.